Albert Einstein

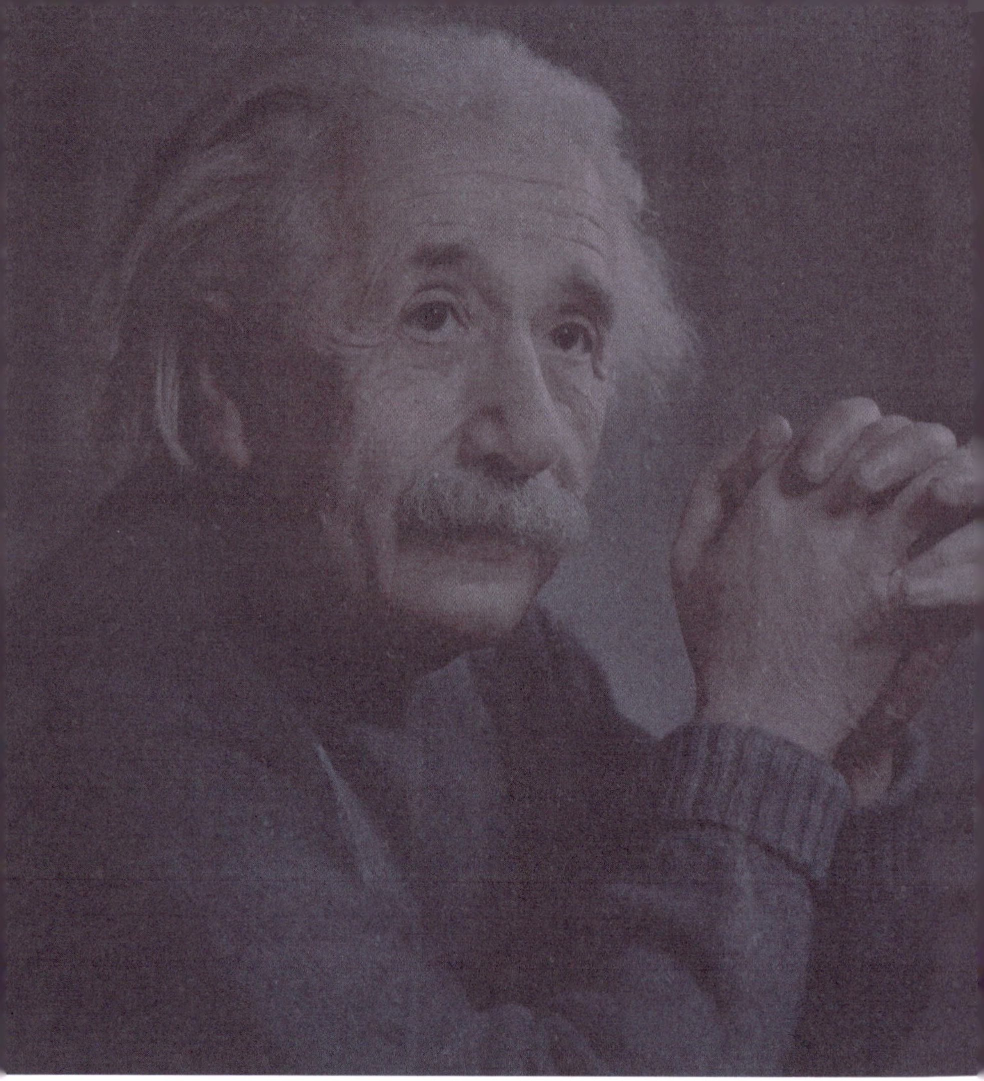

www.pegasusforkids.com

Published by Kuldeep Jain for B. Jain Publishers (P) Ltd., D-157, Sector 63, Noida - 201307, U.P

Registered office: 1921/10, Chuna Mandi, Paharganj, New Delhi-110055

Printed in India

Contents

5 Who was Albert Einstein?

6 Early Life

14 The Elementary School Years

17 The Gymnasium Years

25 Later Years of Education

29 Albert Enters Family Life

33 'Miracle' Year

37 Theory of Relativity

43 Shifting to the United States

49 Final Years

55 Timeline

60 Activities

62 Glossary

Who was Albert Einstein?

Albert Einstein was a German-born physicist who developed the 'Theory of Relativity'. He is considered to be the most prominent physicist of the 20th century.

Born in Ulm, Württemberg, Germany in 1879, Einstein developed the 'Special and General Theories of Relativity', which showed how the speed at which time happens is mutable; that space and time are not discrete entities: time and space and motion (i.e. movement through space) collapse into a fourth dimension, in which all act on each other. Einstein's theory was based on two key principles:

- The principle of relativity: The laws of physics never change, even for objects moving in inertial (constant speed) frames of reference.
- The principle of the speed of light: The speed of light is the same for all observers, regardless of their motion relative to the light source.

In 1921, Einstein won the Nobel Prize for physics for his explanation of the photoelectric effect. Einstein is generally considered as the most influential physicist of the 20th century. He died on April 18, 1955, in Princeton, New Jersey.

Early Life

Albert Einstein was born on March 14, 1879 in Ulm, Württemberg, Germany. He grew up in a secular, middle-class Jewish family. His father, Hermann Einstein, was a salesperson and an engineer. He along with his brother founded Elektrotechnische Fabrik J. Einstein & Cie, a company that manufactured electrical equipment in Munich, Germany. Albert's mother, Pauline Koch, ran the family household.

When Einstein was two-and-a-half years old, his sister Maria Winteler Einstein, commonly known as Maja, was born. Albert, who himself was very young at that time, thought Maja was a new toy to play with, when his parents first introduced her to Einstein. Over the years, Maja became Einstein's constant companion and confidant.

In his childhood days, Einstein was a shy and quiet boy. He did not begin to speak until the age of two. However, even when he began to speak, he would quietly rehearse what he wanted to say before sharing his thoughts with others.

This unusual behaviour and lack of confidence in voicing his thoughts and opinions made his teachers question his academic ability. They believed him to be a slow learner rather than a gifted child. Even outside of his academic circle, Einstein lacked social skills and would rarely mix up with people. He would spend most of his time by himself and would spend hours making constructions, puzzling over jigsaws. This actually brought out the qualities of both persistence and tenacity when he engaged in activities that interested him. He also marvelled at the mysteries

of the world and asked questions about experiences that children his age would rarely ask.

In his later years, Einstein wrote about two 'wonders' that deeply affected his growing-up years. The first was when his father gifted him a compass at age 5. Young Einstein was rather puzzled to see that invisible forces could move the needle of the compass. This incident later led to his lifelong fascination with invisible forces. The second wonder came at the age of 12, when he discovered a book of geometry— Euclid's Elements. He read the book with immense passion, calling it his 'sacred little geometry book'. By the age of twelve, Einstein had taught himself Euclidean geometry with only the help of a school booklet, and then moved on to calculus.

As a child, when he played games with his sister and cousins, he was invariably given the role of a referee as he had a highly developed sense of justice. At the age of five, Einstein's parents appointed a tutor whose job was to prepare him for the rigours of school. Naturally, his tutoring sessions went on exactly the way he would be taught at school (mechanical rote learning). But this did not continue for long and the tutor left soon due to the temper tantrums of young Einstein. Even as a pre-schooler, Einstein showed an aversion to rote learning and would often tell people around him to understand

that mechanical learning was not for him. Einstein attended elementary school at the Luitpold Gymnasium in Munich. However, he felt a sense of alienation there and struggled with the school's rigid pedagogical style. He also had what were considered to be speech and language problems, anti-social tendencies and behavioural issues, though he developed a passion for classical music and playing the violin that would stay with him into his later years. Nevertheless, Einstein's youth was marked by deep inquisitiveness and inquiry.

His mother, Pauline, was an accomplished pianist. She started imparting violin lessons to her son. Initially, Einstein hated playing the violin. However, when he turned 13, he quickly changed his mind about violin when he heard the music of Mozart. With a new passion and enthusiasm, Einstein continued to play the violin until the last few years of his life.

The Elementary School Years

Einstein entered Peterschule, a Catholic elementary school, near his home. Although the school had students from all socio-economic groups, Einstein was the only Jew. His teachers were considered to have liberal views regarding the religion of the students.

Einstein was generally a well-behaved boy at the elementary school and often ranked at the top of his class, thus making his parents proud of their son. As his elementary years passed, Einstein gradually lost interest in studies and fared poorly. During his third year at school, he was moved from Form IIIA to Form IIIB due to a temper tantrum that he had shown. It was apparent from his behaviour

that he was frustrated. Einstein had stated that he saw his teachers at the elementary school as drill sergeants and his teachers at the Gymnasium (German High School) as lieutenants.

The focus of education at that time was rote learning and memorization. This acted as a hindrance to his creative thoughts and denied him the opportunity to explore the subject that fascinated him.

The Gymnasium Years

Einstein's elementary school years were relatively uneventful. However, the situation changed soon after, when he joined the Luitpold Gymnasium at nine-and-a-half years of age. Although it was universally acknowledged that the school was 'enlightened' and 'progressive' (since it included 3-4 hours a week spent on mathematics and science instruction), the majority of time was still spent on the traditional subjects of Latin and Greek.

Einstein was extremely good at logical-mathematical and visual-spatial areas. He had the ability to visualize problems and solutions. Although he maintained passing grades, he found memorizing texts a difficult task. The curriculum provided few opportunities for the subjects he was good at, as physics did not even appear in the curriculum until the seventh year.

Years later, researchers feel that Einstein's originality of thought, flexibility in thinking, inquisitiveness, imagination and complexity of thought were characteristics of an extremely gifted child. Had his teachers recognized his skill and passion for mathematics and science, they would have acknowledged Einstein not only as a lesson learner, but a producer of new knowledge at a much younger age! It is also thought that had Einstein got the opportunity for flexible teaching and a modified curriculum, he would have secured remarkable scores at school instead of being dismissed as an underachiever.

Instead of appreciating his curiosity, his teachers resisted him. They believed that he was challenging their authority and that he had little respect for them. Einstein could not understand their blind faith in the knowledge that had been handed down from generation to generation without being questioned.

It was at this phase that Einstein was saved by the mentors he had outside school. The first of these was his uncle Jakob, who was an engineer by profession. He had introduced Einstein to the wonders of algebra and Pythagoras' theorem. Einstein was so fascinated by this mathematical concept that he spent full three weeks developing a proof for the theory by himself! Although Einstein's proof was not original, it was unique to him.

His second mentor was Max Talmud, a Russian-German medical student with whom his family became friendly in the year 1889. Talmud's mentorship was remarkable in providing the mathematics challenge to Einstein, which the latter was lacking in school. He gave Einstein a series of mathematics textbooks that the young boy would spend hours working through independently. Einstein would also share his solutions with his mentor once a week.

A crucial turning point occurred when Einstein turned 16. Talmud had introduced him to a children's science series by Aaron Bernstein. The book was called *Naturwissenschaftliche Volksbucher* (1867–68; Popular Books on Physical Science), in which the author imagined riding alongside electricity that was travelling inside a telegraph wire!

Einstein began to wonder what a light beam would look like if one could run alongside it at the same speed. If light was a wave, then the light beam should appear stationary, just like a frozen wave. Yet, in reality, the light beam would be moving. Even as a child, Einstein knew that stationary light waves have never been seen and that there was some mystery to this phenomenon. This mystery led him to write his first scientific paper at the age of 16. The paper was titled, 'The Investigation of the State of Aether in Magnetic Fields.' This question of the relative speed to an observer who is not moving and the observer moving with the light was a question that dominated his thinking for the next 10 years.

Later Years of Education

In 1894, Einstein's father's company failed to get an important contract to supply electricity to the city of Munich, thus forcing him to move his family to Milan in Italy. Einstein was left at a relative's boarding house in Munich to finish his education at the Luitpold Gymnasium. He was miserable, lonely and was always in fear of being forced into military duty as he was approaching 16 years of age.

As a result, Einstein withdrew from school, using a doctor's note to excuse himself on the pretext of overtiredness. After being excused from school, he made his way to Milan to join his parents. His parents sympathized with him, but were concerned about the problems that he would face as a school

dropout and draft dodger with no skills that would fetch him an appropriate job.

However, as luck would have it, Einstein was able to apply directly to the Eidgenössische Polytechnische Schule (Swiss Federal Polytechnic School) in Zürich, Switzerland. As he lacked the equivalent of a high school diploma, he failed in clearing the entrance exam. Nevertheless, he scored exceptional marks in mathematics and physics. This cleared his way to the polytechnic school, provided he completed his formal schooling first.

Einstein went to a special high school run by Jost Winteler in Aarau, Switzerland. He was finally in a school that fostered his creative productive giftedness. After finishing at Aarau, Einstein once again applied to Zurich Polytechnic and was accepted. Finally, he graduated in 1896 at age 17.

Einstein became lifelong friends with the Winteler family, with whom he had been boarding. At this time, Einstein renounced his German citizenship to avoid military service and enrolled at the Zurich school.

Albert Enters Family Life

Einstein would fondly remember his years in Zurich as some of the happiest days of his life. He met many students who would go on to become his loyal friends, such as Marcel Grossmann, a mathematician, and Michele Besso, with whom he enjoyed lengthy conversations about space and time. He also met his future wife, Mileva Maric, a fellow physics student from Serbia.

After graduating from the polytechnic institute, Einstein faced a series of difficulties over the next few years. As he

liked to study on his own, he did not attend classes. This gave rise to a sense of enmity with some of his professors. One of his professors in particular, Heinrich Weber, wrote a letter of recommendation at Einstein's request that nearly ruined his future. Due to this letter, Einstein was turned down from every academic position that he applied for after graduation!

Meanwhile, Einstein's relationship with Mileva deepened, but his parents strongly opposed the relationship. This was because of her Serbian background. However, Einstein defied his parents and continued to meet Mileva.

At this point perhaps, he had reached the lowest phase of his life. He could not marry Mileva and support a family without a job. On the other hand, his father's business had gone bankrupt. At this time, Einstein took lowly jobs like tutoring children as he had become desperate and unemployed. But he was unable to hold on to any of them.

A turning point came in 1902, when the father of his lifelong friend, Marcel Grossman, recommended him for a position as a clerk in the Swiss patent office in Bern, Switzerland. Einstein's father became seriously ill about the same time. Just before he died, he gave his blessings for Einstein to marry Mileva. With a meagre but steady income, Einstein married Mileva on January 6, 1903. In May 1904, they welcomed their first son, Hans Albert. Their second son, Eduard, was born in 1910.

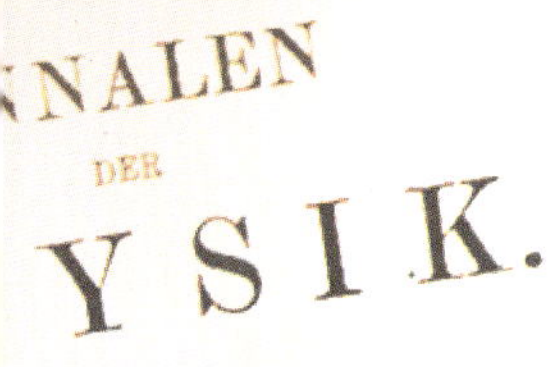

'Miracle' Year

While working at the patent office, Einstein did some of the most creative work of his life. He produced four remarkable articles in 1905 alone.

In 1905, often called Einstein's 'miracle year', he submitted a paper for his doctorate and had four papers published in the *Annalen der Physik*, one of the best known journals on physics. The four papers were the photoelectric effect, Brownian motion, special relativity, and the equivalence of

matter and energy. All of these would change the course of modern physics and make Einstein well known in the academic world.

In the beginning, Einstein's 1905 papers were ignored by the scientists of the physics community. However, things took a turn for the good when he received the attention of Max Planck, who was perhaps the most influential physicist of his generation and founder of the 'Quantum Theory' (theoretical basis of modern physics that explains the nature and behaviour of matter and energy on the atomic and subatomic level). When Planck began paying complimentary comments on Einstein's work and his experiments that confirmed his theories, Einstein was invited to present his lecture at international meetings and he rose rapidly in the academic world. He was offered a series of positions at prestigious institutions, including the University of Zürich, the University of Prague, the Swiss Federal Institute of Technology, and finally the University of Berlin, where he served as the director of the Kaiser Wilhelm Institute for Physics from 1913 to 1933.

As his fame spread, Einstein' personal life suffered a setback. His constant travel and intense study for his work, coupled with low financial status gave rise to several arguments with his wife. All these happenings led Einstein to believe that his marriage was over. He finally divorced Mileva in 1919.

Even while he was married to Mileva, Einstein developed romantic connections with his distant cousin, Elsa. Hence, soon after his separation with Mileva, he married Elsa in 1919. Elsa was priceless to her brilliant husband's career in physics, managing his day-to-day life and nursing him in poor health. When the Nazi movement forced them to leave Germany, Elsa and Einstein moved to Princeton, New Jersey, where Elsa died in 1936.

Theory of Relativity

In November 1915, Einstein, who was still working as a clerk in a Swiss patent office, realized that Newton's 'Law of Gravity' was incorrect when talking about very large and very distant objects. He, therefore, revised Newton's laws of gravity to make them more accurate. We call what he developed, 'Theory of Relativity' as Einstein's best work in the field of physics! He was convinced that general relativity was correct.

The Theory of Relativity is based on two premises. The first is called 'Special Relativity'. This theory states that it is impossible to determine whether or not you are moving unless you look at another object. If you were in the middle of outer space, far from any other objects, how would you know whether or not you were moving? All movement is relative to other objects.

Relative to the Earth, most meteorites move at about 40,233 km per hour. But if you were standing on a meteorite looking at another meteorite going in the same direction as you at the same speed, it would not appear to move at all!

Special Relativity also states that the speed of light is always constant. This means that no matter what you do to light, it will always travel at the same speed. Scientists are still finding ways to learn how to make light travel faster, but there is still a long way to go.

The 'Theory of General Relativity' is the one which has redefined the laws of gravity. It says that it is impossible to tell the difference between gravity and the force of inertia of a moving object.

In other words, if you climb inside a spinning spacecraft, the inertia will force you to move towards the outside walls in a way that would feel just like gravity. This explains why future spacecraft designs often have large spinning cylinders attached to them.

In the year 1921, Einstein received the Nobel Prize for Physics. As relativity was still considered a subject on which scientists argued, Einstein received the award for his explanation of the photoelectric effect.

In the 1920s, Einstein launched the new science of cosmology. His equations predicted that the universe is active, ever expanding or contracting. This was against the prevalent view that the universe was static; a view that Einstein also held earlier.

However, his later calculations in the general theory indicated that the universe could be expanding or contracting. In 1929, Edwin Hubble, the famous American astronomer, found that the universe was indeed expanding, thereby confirming Einstein's work.

In 1930, during a visit to the Mount Wilson Observatory near Los Angeles, Einstein met Hubble and admitted that his original theory (stating that the size and shape of the universe was unchanging) was his 'greatest blunder'.

While Einstein was touring the world speaking on his theories in the 1920s, the Nazis gained power under the leadership of Adolph Hitler. As is known to the world, Hitler had a great dislike for the Jews; and Einstein was believed to be a Jew by many people. As a consequence, his theories on relativity became an easy target of the Nazis.

In 1931, the Nazis forced other physicists to publicly announce that Einstein's theories were 'evil' or 'Jewish physics'. At this time, Einstein learned that the new German government, then in full control of the Nazi party, had passed a law stating that Jews could not hold any official position, including teaching at universities. Einstein also learned that his name was on a list of killing targets. A Nazi organization had published a magazine with Einstein's picture and the caption, 'Not Yet Hanged,' on the cover.

Shifting to the United States

A longtime pacifist and a Jew, Einstein became a target of hostility in Weimar Germany. The Germans were already facing economic turmoil in the aftermath of defeat in the Great War. In December 1932, a month before Hitler took to the chair of the chancellor of Germany, Einstein made the decision to immigrate to the United States. There he took a position at the newly founded Institute for Advanced Study in Princeton, New Jersey. He never again returned to the country of his birth. The Institute for Advanced Study at Princeton, New Jersey soon became an important place of visit for physicists from around the world. It was here that Einstein would spend the rest of his career trying to develop an all-embracing theory that would unify the forces of the universe, and thereby the laws of physics, into one framework. Other than Einstein, many other European scientists also fled from various countries threatened by Nazi takeover and set their base in the United States. Some of these scientists knew of Nazi plans to develop an atomic weapon. They had even warned Washington, D.C., but their warnings were not taken seriously.

In the summer of 1939, Einstein, at the urging of the Hungarian physicist Leo Szilard, wrote a letter to President Franklin D. Roosevelt. In that letter, Einstein apprised the President of the possibility of the Nazis of developing a bomb. President Roosevelt could not risk the possibility that Germany might develop an atomic bomb first. This letter is believed to be the key factor that motivated the United States to develop nuclear weapons. Roosevelt soon invited Einstein to meet him and the United States initiated the 'Manhattan Project'.

In 1935, Einstein was granted permanent residency in the United States and he became an American citizen in 1940. As the Manhattan Project was gradually developed from drawing board to testing and development at Los Alamos, New Mexico, many of Einstein's colleagues were asked to develop the first atomic bomb. However, Einstein did not take part in its implementation due to his pacifist and social affiliations. He also ended up earning much scrutiny and distrust from Federal Bureau of Investigation (FBI) director J. Edgar Hoover.

According to many researchers, the reason for not including Einstein was that the U.S. government thought he would not like the idea of developing a bomb due to his lifelong association with peace and socialist organizations.

Nevertheless, during the World War, Einstein helped the U.S. Navy evaluate designs for future weapon systems. He also contributed to the war effort by auctioning off his priceless personal manuscripts. One such example was a handwritten copy of his 1905 paper on 'Special Relativity', which sold for US$ 6.5 million, and is now preserved in the Library of Congress.

While on vacation, on August 6, 1945, Einstein heard the news of an atomic bomb being dropped on Hiroshima, Japan. He soon became involved in an international effort to try to bring the atomic bomb under control. In 1946, he formed the Emergency Committee of Atomic Scientists with physicist Szilard. In 1947, in an article that he wrote for *The Atlantic Monthly*, Einstein argued that the United States should not try to monopolize the atomic bomb but, instead, should supply the United Nations with nuclear weapons for the sole purpose of maintaining a preventive for future wars.

It was around the same time that Einstein also became a member of the National Association for the Advancement of Colored People, taking into consideration the parallels between the treatment of Jews in Germany and African Americans in the United States. He collaborated with scholar and activist W.E.B. Du Bois as well as performing artist Paul Robeson to campaign for civil rights, calling racism a "disease" in a 1946 Lincoln University speech. The following speech received widespread applause and reflected Einstein's great courage in showing and doing what most others of his time wouldn't dare to.

"There is … a somber point in the social outlook of Americans … Their sense of equality and human dignity is mainly limited to men of white. Even among these there are prejudices of which I as a Jew am dearly conscious;

but they are unimportant in comparison with the attitude of 'Whites' toward their fellow-citizens of darker complexion, particularly toward Negroes. … The more I feel an American, the more this situation pains me. I can escape the feeling of complicity in it only by speaking out."

After the Second World War, Einstein continued to work on many important aspects of the Theory of General Relativity. Nevertheless, he became increasingly isolated from the rest of the physics community, as majority of scientists were working on the quantum theory, not on relativity.

Final Years

Einstein spent the last three decades of his life vainly struggling to formulate what he called a 'unified field theory'. This was his vision of a single mathematical model that could explain all the laws of physics. However, he never found his answer. Even today, after half a century of Einstein's death, scientists continue to search for this model of theoretical physics. Although Einstein was not successful in his unified field work, his fame and status as a pure genius continued to grow.

In his later years, Einstein continued to talk on all such social and political issues which he thought to be wrong. He was unafraid to stand against the ways of that time. All these activities made the authorities of America deeply suspicious of him. The FBI opened a file on Einstein, and it soon spanned nearly 1,500 pages.

Einstein was proud to serve with some of the world's most accomplished Jews, including philosopher Martin Buber, psychologist Sigmund Freud, and first Israeli President Chaim Weizmann on the First Board of Governors of the Hebrew University of Jersusalem, which had been founded in the early 1920s.

When Weizmann passed away in 1952, Ben-Gurion offered the Israeli presidency (a largely ceremonial position) to Einstein, who was described in an Israeli newspaper at the time as 'the greatest Jew alive'.

Einstein expressed his feelings thus:

"I am deeply moved by the offer from our State of Israel, and at once saddened and ashamed that I cannot accept it."

This was because Einstein had no desire to spend his last years as a politician.

On April 17, 1955, while working on a speech on the occasion of Israel's seventh anniversary, Einstein suffered an abdominal aortic aneurysm and experienced an internal bleeding. He was taken to the University Medical Centre at Princeton for treatment. But Einstein refused to be operated saying that he had lived his life and was content to accept his fate. Einstein ensured immense pain in the last days of his life and required frequent sedatives.

"I want to go when I want," he stated at the time. "It is tasteless to prolong life artificially. I have done my share, it is time to go. I will do it elegantly."

Einstein died at the University Medical Centre early the very next morning on April 18, 1955. He was 76.

The autopsy of Einstein was conducted at Princeton Hospital. During the autopsy, Thomas Stoltz Harvey removed Einstein's brain, reportedly without the permission of his family. He did so for preservation and future study by doctors of neuroscience. Dr. Harvey sectioned the preserved brain into 170 pieces in a lab, a

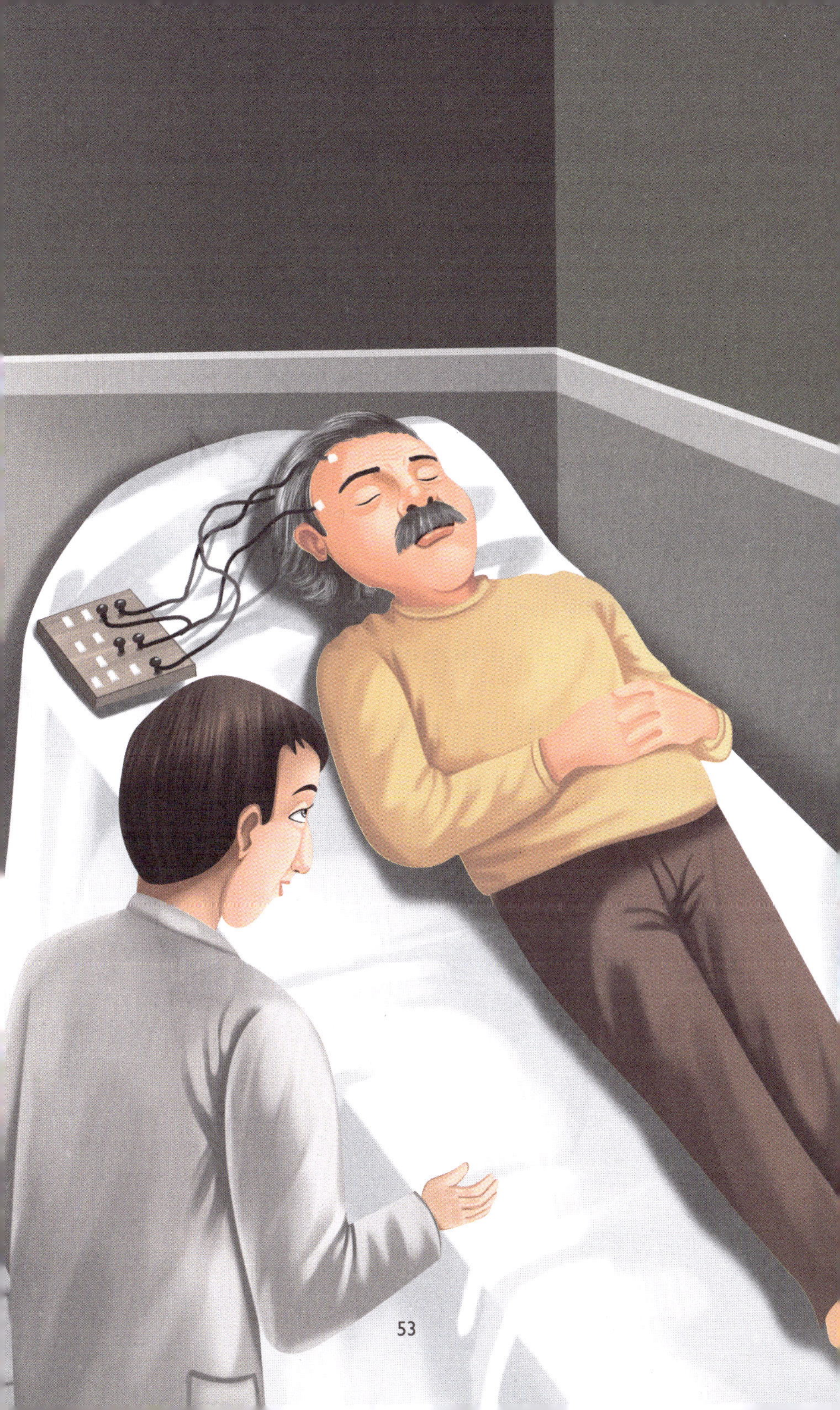

process that took three full months to complete. Harvey retained two complete sets of Einstein's brain for his own research and distributed the rest to handpicked leading pathologists of the time.

Strict privacy was maintained at the cremation of Einstein, at the Ewing Cemetery crematorium in West Trenton. Following his wishes, no religious services were held and his ashes were scattered in an undisclosed location. Present at the cremation were about a dozen scientists, his close friends and his son, Dr. Hans Albert Einstein, professor of engineering at California Institute of Technology.

Einstein's story can be best summed up through one of his own quotes about himself:

**"I have no special talents.
I am only passionately curious."**

Timeline

- 1879 Albert Einstein was born in Ulm, Germany.
- 1880 The family moves to Munich.
- 1881 His sister Maja (Maria) is born.
- 1884 When he was only four years old, his father gave him a pocket compass and he was fascinated by the thought that some invisible, unseen power was moving the needle.
- 1889 Einstein is introduced to his mentor Max Talmud. He also attends the Luitpold-Gymnasium in Munich for the next six years.
- 1894 Due to financial reasons, the Einstein family moves from Munich to Pavia, Italy. Einstein is left in Munich to finish his studies but soon decides to follow the family to Italy.
- 1895 He is sent to the Swiss town of Aarau to finish high school.
- 1896 Einstein graduates from high school at the age of 17 and enrolls at the ETH (the Federal Polytechnic) in Zurich. He gives up his German citizenship.
- 1898 He meets and falls in love with Mileva Maric, a fellow physicist.

- 1900 Einstein graduates in 1900 from ETH with a degree in physics.
- 1903 Einstein marries Mileva Maric.
- 1904 Einstein and Mileva's first son, Hans Albert Einstein, is born in Berne, Switzerland.
- 1905 Einstein formulates his 'Special Theory of Relativity'.
- 1907 Einstein begins applying the laws of gravity to his Special Theory of Relativity.
- 1908 He becomes an associate professor at the University of Bern.
- 1909 He resigns from Patent Office and is appointed Associate Professor of theoretical physics at Zurich University.
- 1910 Einstein and Mileva's second son, Eduard, is born in Munich. Einstein writes a paper on critical opalescence that described why the sky is blue.
- 1911 Einstein predicts bending of light. He is appointed Professor of theoretical physics at the German University of Prague.
- 1913 He is appointed professor of theoretical physics at the Federal Institute of

Technology, Zurich and works on his new Theory of Gravity.

- **1914** Albert and Mileva separate and live apart. Einstein is appointed professor at University of Berlin.

  World War I begins. Einstein signs anti-war 'Manifesto to Europeans'.

- **1915** Einstein completes the General Theory of Relativity.
- **1916** His General Theory of Relativity is published.
- **1917** Einstein writes his first paper on cosmology. He is appointed the Director of Kaiser Wilhelm Institute for Physics in Berlin.
- **1918** Einstein falls seriously ill and is nursed by his cousin, Elsa Einstein Loewenthal.
- **1919** Einstein and Mileva get divorced and he marries his cousin Elsa on May 29 the same year. A solar eclipse proves Einstein's General Theory of Relativity.
- **1921** Einstein visits the U.S. and lectures at Princeton University on the Theory of Relativity.
- **1922** Einstein is awarded the Nobel Prize in physics for the year 1921.

Timeline

- 1928 Einstein begins pursing his idea of a unified field theory. He becomes ill and is diagnosed with the enlargement of the heart.
- 1930– 1933 Einstein makes several visits to the USA delivering lectures at various universities.
- 1933 Adolf Hitler is appointed Chancellor of Germany.

  Einstein leaves Germany and emigrates to U.S. in September. He settles down at Princeton, New Jersey where he assumes a post at the Institute for Advanced Study.
- 1936 Elsa Einstein dies.
- 1939 World War II begins and Einstein, at the urging of the Hungarian physicist Leo Szilard, warns President Roosevelt that Germany might build an atomic bomb. He then recommends nuclear research.
- 1940 Einstein becomes a citizen of the United States but also retains his Swiss citizenship.
- 1943 Einstein begins working with the Research and Development Division of the U.S. Navy on Ammunition and Explosives.

- 1945 World War II ends with the terrible nuclear bombing of Hiroshima and Nagasaki.
- 1946 Einstein is appointed chairman of the Emergency Committee for Atomic Scientists.
- 1947 He works on behalf of the cause for disarmament.
- 1949 Mileva dies.
- 1952 Einstein is offered presidency of the State of Israel.
- 1955 Einstein co-signs the Russell-Einstein Manifesto warning of the nuclear threat.

  He experiences internal bleeding.

  Einstein dies in Princeton Hospital at the age of 76.

Activities

Class Discussion

- Discuss the difference between an 'invention' and 'discovery' with the help of your teacher.
- Who is an inventor? Discuss about a few inventors and their inventions.

Group Activity

Make a project on any one

- Rain
- Wind
- Any one scientist
- Formation of day and night

Be prepared adequately so that you can explain what you have done.

Questions

1. When and where was Einstein born?
2. What were the names of his parents?
3. What was the name of his younger sister?
4. Describe the childhood nature of Einstein
5. Which musical instrument did Einstein play when he was 13 years of age?

6. Which were the two schools that Albert went to as a child?
7. Which were his favourite subjects?
8. Why do you think Einstein disliked the system of education in his schools?
9. Name the two mentors Einstein was blessed with
10. Do you remember the name of his first wife?
11. Which theory was Albert trying to formulate?
12. Why did Einstein move away from Germany to United States permanently?
13. When did Albert get the Nobel Prize and for what?
14. Who was the Nazi leader who hated Albert and why?
15. In which place did Einstein live in United States?
16. Name the disease by which finally Albert died?
17. Why do you think scientists preserved his brain?

Glossary

abdominal aortic aneurysm: a localized enlargement of the abdominal aorta such that the diameter is greater than 3 cm or more than 50 percent larger than normal

atomic bomb: a nuclear explosive

auctioning: a public sale in which goods or property are sold to the highest bidder

bankrupt: a person who has run out of money and is unable to pay debts

complimentary: praising or approving

confidant: A person with whom one shares a secret

constructions: to build something large

cosmology: the science which tells about the origin and development of the universe

curriculum: the subjects comprising a course of study in a school or college

enlightened: showing a rational and modern outlook

equation: a mathematical statement

exceptional: unusual

frozen: having turned into ice as a result of extreme cold

gravity: the force that attracts a body towards the centre of the Earth

inertia: a property of matter by which it continues in its existing state of rest or uniform motion in a straight line until forced to move or stop

influential: having great influence on someone or something:

inquisitiveness: having interest in learning things

liberal: a person who is willing to respect or accept behaviour or opinions of others

Manhattan Project: a research and development project that produced the first nuclear weapons during World War II; it was led by the United States

marvelled: Be filled with astonishment:

mechanical: relating to machines

memorization: learn by heart:

miracle: a remarkable event

miserable: unhappy or uncomfortable

nazi: followers of Nazism begun by the German dictator Hitler

overtiredness: too much tired

Glossary

persistence: The fact of continuing in an opinion or course of action irrespective of opposition

physicist: an expert in or student of physics

prestigious: having high status

progressive: developing gradually or in stages

recommended: to put forward someone or something with approval

rehearse: the practice of a play, piece of music, or other work for public performance:

secular: Not connected with any religious or spiritual matters

sedatives: a drug taken to induce sleep

spinning: the action of spinning or the conversion of fibres into yarn

sympathized: feeling or express sympathy

tantrum: An uncontrolled outburst of anger

tenacity: The quality of being able to grip something firmly

underachiever: do less well than expected

visualize: imagine